EVERY DAY IS A GOOD DAY

A DRAMA

By ED STRUM

REMDUST PUBLISHING
Every Day Is A Good Day, Copyright © 2024 by Ed Strum
All Rights Reserved
ISBN 978-0-9913897-6-6

CAUTION: Professionals and amateurs are hereby warned that EVERY DAY IS A GOOD DAY is subject to a royalty. It is fully protected under the copyright laws of the United States of America, and of all countries covered by the International Copyright Union (including the Dominion of Canada and the rest of the British Commonwealth), and of all countries covered by the Pan-American Copyright Convention and the Universal Copyright Convention, and of all countries with which the United States has reciprocal copyright relations. All rights including professional, amateur, motion picture, recitation, lecturing, public reading, radio broadcasting, television, video or sound taping, all other forms of mechanical or electronic reproductions, such as information storage and retrieval systems and photocopying, and the rights of translation into foreign languages, are strictly reserved. Permission must be secured from the author's Agent in writing. This copyright applies to all versions of the play and the screenplay written by this author. The English language stage and amateur performance rights are controlled exclusively by REMDUST PUBLISHING. No professional or non-professional performance of the play, or reading, may be given without obtaining in advance the written permission of REMDUST PUBLISHING or the author, and paying the requisite fee.

Inquiries concerning all rights should be addressed to REMDUST PUBLISHING (Remdustpublishing@yahoo.com), 445 Deerfield Circle, Santa Rosa, CA 95409.

This is a work of fiction. No character in this dramatic play represents any individual person, living or dead.

DEDICATED TO THE MEMORY

Of

Edward A. Strum (1909 to 1971)

IN REMEMBRANCE OF

TOM and ERNEST and VAN and SKIP and PAM and PAUL and SUE and SHARON and DAVE and BILL and TOM and so many others.

May You Forever Be In Our Hearts and Minds and Voices

Books by Ed Strum

THE CONNOISSSEURS – A Play

MONTOBA – A Novel

THE BURROW & THE GREAT PANDEMIC, A Play

JOURNEY OF THE SCROLLS – A Novel

JOURNEY OF THE SCROLLS – SPECIAL EDITION

THE PRINCESS OF ÉLEVÉ – A Play

EVERY DAY IS A GOOD DAY – A Drama

THE HOLLOW PENCIL – A Play

CASCADIA and THE GREAT PANDEMIC – A Novel

ADAM'S ARK & THE GREAT PANDEMIC – A Play

RICHIE – A Poetic Play in One Scene

A SENSORY FEAST – An Anthology of Prose Poetry

Acknowledgements

Many thanks to Ann and Tom Clemo for the first reading of the play. I extend my appreciation to Merritt Olsen for his comments, and to Leslie Brown, Heather Couthaud, Sandra Geist, and Jim Jacobs for their reviews and comments.

My thanks to the reading group (Warren Baehr, Gray Cope, Julie Laidlaw, Stan Matthews, Maureen See, and Janet Thomas) for readings of the full play, their support and comments, and my thanks to Gail Leschine-Seitz for her comments and suggestions.

EVERY DAY

IS

A GOOD DAY

EVERY DAY IS A GOOD DAY

CAST OF CHARACTERS
(In order of appearance)

Todd

Charlie – older than Deidre

Willie – older than Charlie

Deidre – 50s

Ensemble (Minimum two actors, women or men): Todd, Nurse, Passersby, Actor, Waitress/Waiter, People in Coffee Shop, Renée.

The action takes place in a hospital room, a park bench, and a coffee shop. It begins sometime in 2016.

Running time: 100 minutes without intermission.

Prologue   *Hospital Room*
ACT ONE   – *Scene One: Park Bench – Several weeks later*
                 Scene Two: Park Bench – Several months later
                 Scene Three: Coffee shop – Same day
ACT TWO   – *Scene One: Coffee shop – Several months later*
                 Scene Two: Park Bench – Same day
                 Scene Three: Coffee shop – Several months later
                 Scene Four: Coffee shop – Next Morning

EVERY DAY IS A GOOD DAY

PROLOGUE

Todd sits upright in the hospital bed, dozing off. He's thin and tired. Charlie enters. He's dressed casually. Dim light enters from direction of window. The sound of light rain comes from outside.

CHARLIE
I found the nurse. She'll be here in a minute.

TODD
More pills and shots and blood draws – it's endless.

CHARLIE
They've got their job to do. Don't they help? The pills and shots?

TODD
A little bit I guess, but it's a waste of time.

Silence. Charlie moves toward the window and looks out.

CHARLIE
I remember when I was directing some play. I've forgotten which one. I was searching for odds and ends. Props, gels, lekos, gobos, extra lighting instruments, stools – you had stuff everywhere.

TODD
(*Smiles.*) Prop room overflowed. Used every corner I could find.

CHARLIE
My key opened every little room. Must have been a dozen of them.

TODD
And you found what you needed?

CHARLIE
Eventually. I remember the first time you took me up to the catwalks to set up lighting instruments.

TODD
I thought you needed an education - if you were going to be a good director. Most aren't interested, but you were.

CHARLIE
You explained about the circuits we had and the different instruments and how we used them. Gels and focusing.

TODD
You really paid attention. You've learned to use lighting with imagination. Terrific. You're quite visual.

CHARLIE
I learned from a great director, and you. Art taught me how to read a script in terms of lighting.

TODD
I can tell.

CHARLIE
When I learned about lighting instruments and options from you, I put it to good use.

TODD
We also have great acoustics in the theater.

CHARLIE
I know. When I direct, I sit in different places and listen to the projection of the actors.

TODD
What about sound effects? We have high quality sound equipment.

CHARLIE
The same thing. Art taught me to read a script over and over, find the sounds and where they come from.

Todd drifts off, thinking.

CHARLIE
(Softly.) Todd?

TODD
What?

CHARLIE
I love the catwalks. I've thought I'd write a play about someone living up there, sort of like Phantom of the Opera.

TODD
(Laughs.) You should. Did I ever tell you we once had someone like that? Sleeping and drinking. He hid a sleeping bag in a small room next to the catwalks. He'd creep in and bring it out at night.

CHARLIE
How'd you discover him?

TODD
(Tired.) One time we found an empty bottle. He ran away when he knew it was over.

CHARLIE
Those catwalks are fantastic. So many things you can do with them.

TODD
(Very quietly.) Sometimes I've thought about hiding up there, getting away from things. A wonderful place.

CHARLIE
(Brief silence.) I remember being in a panic during the last week of tech before we opened. It was hell. A disaster. The set. Rehearsals. Lights. But you were always calm. Don't worry, you'd say, it'll all be ready by opening night.

TODD
And was it?

CHARLIE
Always.

TODD

You were pretty calm yourself. Do you remember that one opening night when the sheriff showed up twenty minutes before curtain, looking for the mother of a cast member?

CHARLIE

What a shock! I thought, *what have we done now*?

TODD

Her daughter crashed her car and was in jail on a DUI. When the mother showed up, you sent her to the jail to see her daughter, then scrambled to fill their roles. You were cool. Amazing.

CHARLIE

I remember it vividly. It was the cast that was amazing. They moved roles, learned lines and blocking, all in twenty minutes. Audience didn't know a thing.

TODD

(Quietly.) That show got standing ovations.

CHARLIE

(Long silence. Looks out window. Sound of rain increases.) What a miserable day. Rain, cold. *(Senses silence. Looks back at Todd.)*

TODD

(Calmly, quietly.) Charlie, every day is a good day.

CHARLIE

(Subdued.) You're right.

TODD

(Softly.) Charlie, make every day count. And Charlie?

CHARLIE

Yes?

Charlie slides over to the bed and holds his hand as Todd speaks almost in a whisper, holding back tears.

TODD

Write a good story for me.

CHARLIE

I will, Todd. I will.

Lights fade slowly. As they fade, the nurse enters and moves toward Todd for an injection, pills, and checks IV. Charlie looks out window in growing darkness. A surreal atmosphere.

ACT ONE

Scene One: Several weeks later. A park bench on a warm sunny day. Willie enters sipping a cup of coffee. He sits. Charlie enters.

CHARLIE
Sorry if I'm late. I just got back from seeing Todd. Haven't seen him in a couple of days. We got talking.

WILLIE
No problem. *(Motions him to sit.)* How is he?

CHARLIE
Pretty weak of course, but his mind's sharp. I'm there every day now. I sit with him, we talk, about the theatre.

WILLIE
I don't know how you do it. I feel awkward with people that're really ill. I don't know what to say.

CHARLIE
Take a chance, Willie. Step into his shoes. Put yourself into his mind. Think about how he might feel.

WILLIE
(Shakes his head.) Easy for you. That's hard for me.

CHARLIE
When I was really sick, I thought people shunned me, were afraid to come talk to me. When I reached out, though, they seemed relieved.

WILLIE
I was never afraid to talk to you. When you were ill, before, or after.

CHARLIE
That's different. You're a good friend. You tell me when I'm wrong.

WILLIE
I don't know if you knew but I was really worried about you.

CHARLIE
I knew. You've always thought of others, always been there for them, for me.

WILLIE
So, what's the key? What do you say when someone's really sick?

CHARLIE
Get them to talk about themselves. Most people like to do that.

WILLIE
(He laughs.) I'll go to see Todd. Thanks.

CHARLIE
Good, and don't talk about yourself. So, how are you?

WILLIE
(Hesitates. Distracted.) I feel terrific. I feel very lucky.

Two women walk by, talking as they go.

FIRST WOMAN
It looks as if she'll beat him in the primaries.

SECOND WOMAN
There's always the chance she'll be assassinated.

FIRST WOMAN
That's a terrible thing to say.

SECOND WOMAN
It's happened before. Remember Bobby Kennedy?

They disappear as Charlie stares after them.

CHARLIE
She isn't the only one thinking that.

WILLIE
Did I ever tell you about my friend Deidre?

CHARLIE
(Startled.) I don't think so.

WILLIE
We met years ago in a Master Gardener class. We discovered we both loved to grow things. It was fun.

CHARLIE
And you kept in touch after that?

WILLIE
Actually, soon after that, we found ourselves running alongside each other in a marathon.

CHARLIE
I didn't know that about you. A runner?

WILLIE
Lots of things you don't know about me. Then we met again years later, waiting for a blood draw.

CHARLIE
Not as much fun as running together.

WILLIE
We were both in remission at that point.

CHARLIE
What's she like?

WILLIE
You'd like her. She's so much like you. Loves art, music. Loves to travel. You should meet her.

CHARLIE
If you say so.

WILLIE

You know, Charlie, we've lost so many people. They were here one day, vibrant, alive, full of humor, and humanity. The next day they were gone, stopped in their tracks. Soon they'll become distant memories. I'm afraid they'll all be forgotten, one by one. I fear we'll be forgotten, too. We too will become distant memories.

CHARLIE

The greatest fear of most people in hospice is that: they're afraid they'll be forgotten after they're gone.

WILLIE

See what I mean? Don't you feel that way sometimes?

CHARLIE

Willie, there's no reason for them to become distant memories, or forgotten. If we remember them, talk about them, share our stories and memories, and even write about them, they'll stay with us.

WILLIE

Remember them laughing and happy, or troubled and down?

CHARLIE

That's our job, yours and mine, to keep their legacy alive, who they were and what they did and what they loved.

WILLIE

What about the people who don't want to be remembered? Or family members who want closure? Or those who're glad someone's gone? What about people with negative things to say that aren't even true?

CHARLIE

There's no room for negative words about one that's passed on. Despicable. I believe everyone fears they'll be forgotten. Everyone wants to be remembered, to feel that their lives mattered. *(Intense passion and anger.)* By George, all lives matter, all people matter.

WILLIE

You're right. But I understand the family, or the spouse or caregiver, wanting closure.

CHARLIE
Wanting to feel a comforting, satisfying sense of finality?

WILLIE
Yes, wanting to move on.

CHARLIE
Especially when it's been a long exhausting process.

WILLIE
I don't understand how one's glad when someone's gone. Do you?

CHARLIE
No. There's so much hatred out there. It's hard to understand where it's coming from.

WILLIE
And when we're gone and can no longer tell our stories about them, and share our memories, what then? What happens to their memories then?

CHARLIE
I told Todd I'd write his story. We can hope others continue the memories. Ancient civilizations had an oral tradition, and some Native American tribes, to pass on ancestor stories and legends by telling them over and over.

WILLIE
What would you say about me, Charlie, when I'm no longer here?

CHARLIE
Ah, but you'll always be here, Willie, in our hearts and minds and souls, in our memories. And what would I say? I'd talk about your generosity, your warmth, your talent, and how much you care. I'd even talk about your humor.

WILLIE
(Softly.) I remember the first time we met.

CHARLIE

So do I. Your garden, chickens. I've always loved the land and growing things, but then I saw how much you did as well. But your humor towers over everything. I've liked you ever since.

WILLIE

I think my soul is buried in the soil, waiting for me.

CHARLIE

Let's get off this somber subject. Back to your humor: your dry understated way, your sense of timing. You walk on stage and take over, even the stage of life. You have a unique presence.

WILLIE

Aren't you going to ask what I would say about you?

CHARLIE

I'm afraid to ask.

WILLIE

I'd tell stories about you.

CHARLIE

For instance?

WILLIE

Once, in a musical you dashed off stage to get a prop. You had to get back on stage quickly but the prop had been moved or misplaced.

CHARLIE

The stage manager screwed up.

WILLIE

Anyway, you dashed back on stage and mimed what you would do with the prop. The audience got it and laughed.

CHARLIE

I love community theatre. There's nothing like the love and understanding you get from an audience. Priceless.

WILLIE
Another time you were upstage and carrying on with some antics. The actors down stage were furious.

CHARLIE
The director told me to do that.

WILLIE
Doesn't matter. That was real upstaging. You were hilarious.

CHARLIE
The audience roared.

WILLIE
The actors down stage didn't.

CHARLIE
I guess I shouldn't have milked it.

A person known only to Willie rushes up.

ACTOR
Willie, I'm glad to find you. We've got to get rid of that other guy.

WILLIE
We open in two days. We can't do that. What's wrong?

ACTOR
I don't like the way he's doing his part.

WILLIE
I'm the director and I think he's doing just great. So are you. We're ready to open. Dress rehearsal tomorrow.

ACTOR
To tell you the truth, I don't like the way you direct.

WILLIE
I'm sorry, but this is no time to bring that up.

ACTOR
I'm not doing it unless you replace him.

WILLIE
I don't work that way. If you won't do it, I'll cancel the show.

ACTOR
You can't do that. I've told lots of people about my show.

WILLIE
I don't respond to threats. And dropping out at the last minute? We don't do that. I'll find someone to replace you.

The person moves forward, about to hit Willie. Charlie jumps up to intervene. The person pushes Willie.

ACTOR
How dare you.

Charlie moves forward to restrain the person and Willie moves forward as well. The person steps back and leaves.

CHARLIE
(They sit down again.) What was that all about, Willie?

WILLIE
He's new to acting. Thinks he's pretty good. Actually, he is, but he's also been some trouble to work with.

CHARLIE
You're better off without him.

Then they talk almost as one voice, rapidly, moving closer.

WILLIE
My favorite story is the gun toss. You were knocked to the ground.

CHARLIE
I was black and blue from falling over and over on numerous takes.

WILLIE

As you fell, you were supposed to toss your gun in the air for me to catch. You were wild.

CHARLIE

Didn't I ever get it right?

WILLIE

Never.

They both laugh and laugh, then grow quiet.

CHARLIE

I remember you and the others backstage during rehearsals.

WILLIE

We were plotting.

CHARLIE

You were making plans about what to do if the lead did something.

WILLIE

Well, he did. Remember when he jumped four pages in the script?

CHARLIE

Incredible. An actress was offstage but the dialogue had her onstage.

WILLIE

You got it. We made up dialogue to go back to where we were.

CHARLIE

I can't remember what the lead did.

WILLIE

Just followed us. We got her back on stage, and continued.

CHARLIE

We've had a few situations like that in our many productions together, haven't we?

WILLIE
Lots. That's community theatre. Even professionals have those.

CHARLIE
Not like community theatre. An unmotivated cross or an unresolved gestalt for a professional is a tragedy. I know.

WILLIE
You're kidding? An unmotivated cross for a professional? Never.

CHARLIE
I saw a preview at Oregon Shakespeare Festival once. An actress ran to a corner, unmotivated, because she had to be there. Later I talked to a cast member. He was apologetic about that happening.

WILLIE
Even in a preview?

CHARLIE
Absolutely!

WILLIE
You have to be creative with an unresolved gestalt.

CHARLIE
Remember in that Neil Simon play when someone dropped something downstage in front of a coffee table?

WILLIE
I remember. Barefoot In The Park. It was a napkin.

CHARLIE
The audience kept watching it and stopped listening to the play.

WILLIE
I was offstage.

CHARLIE
You entered from stage left, saw the problem, and solved it.

WILLIE
I picked it up and mopped my brow as if it was designed that way.

CHARLIE
Quick thinking.

WILLIE
The worst thing is dropping lines. How many times have you heard, "Don't worry, I'll have my lines memorized by opening night."?

CHARLIE
Too often. Remember the time a backstage crew changed some tea to some other stuff? What was that?

WILLIE
Yeah. That was terrible. One of the actresses drank it as if it was alcohol. She had a severe reaction and couldn't breathe. *(They grow silent.)* That wasn't funny. I don't think the audience knew.

CHARLIE
And celebrations backstage? Trying different kinds of scotch?

WILLIE
The play involved drinking scotch as I remember, so the cast sometimes brought real stuff to drink afterwards.

CHARLIE
No harm in celebrating afterwards, is there? We all work hard to put on a performance.

WILLIE
Some community theatre actors think a little bit to drink relaxes them, improves their performance.

CHARLIE
Are you telling me they drink before the play?

WILLIE
Yep. Once in a while. During it also. I'm ashamed to admit I did it a couple of times.

CHARLIE
Did it? Improve your performance, that is?

WILLIE
Are you kidding? I was terrible but thought I was good.

CHARLIE
And the other dressing room story? About the actress that loved to come into the men's dressing room.

WILLIE
You seem to remember a lot.

CHARLIE
Why did she?

WILLIE
Do I have to spell it out?

There is an awkward silence, then they continue.

CHARLIE
I directed a play once where one of the two actors got lost and kept going around and around.

WILLIE
What did the other actor do?

CHARLIE
He was dumbfounded and just went along for the ride. I was in stitches. I don't think the audience noticed.

WILLIE
Don't be so sure. Audiences are smarter than you might think.

CHARLIE
Remember the Tennessee Williams. The actress and actor got lost and went all over the place, back and forth.

17

WILLIE
Going here and there just putting out lines. I remember watching.

CHARLIE
It was both tragic and hilarious. They'd never learned their lines. Eventually they found a way out of the mess.

WILLIE
(Their laughter slows.) The audience knew what was happening.

CHARLIE
They sure did. The word spread on the street and they stopped coming to see the show.

WILLIE
(Quietly.) We've had some great times together, Charlie.

CHARLIE
We sure have. You said you were afraid to go up to someone you know who's obviously sick. When I'd lost a lot of weight, I looked like a scarecrow. I was paranoid about what people were thinking. I honestly wasn't sure I'd survive and felt as if people were just waiting for the end, even hoping I would go soon. Terrible thoughts. But I survived and grew stronger. Now lots of people come up and all say the same thing: that I look great or something similar.

A person they both know walks by and stops briefly.

MAN/WOMAN
Hi, Willie. *(With more enthusiasm. Shakes Charlie's hand.)* Hey, Charlie. I haven't seen you for a long time. You're looking really great. Are you doing anything at the theatre?

CHARLIE
No, not for now. Maybe one of these days. Good to see you. *(The person exits.)* See what I mean. For whatever reason people are not comfortable with talking to those who are ill and possibly terminal. They don't want to say you look good. That's a lie. When you improve they say you look terrific but they're also saying you used to look like crap.

WILLIE

Well, I guess you used to look like crap, Charlie.

CHARLIE

And I guess you must look like crap now, Willie, from the reaction.

WILLIE

I guess I should tell you the truth about me and my health. I don't feel right.

CHARLIE

What's wrong?

WILLIE

I don't know. I had some blood tests done some time ago and then they wanted more. Then another set and a long wait while different doctors looked at results. They wanted to be certain. I'm still waiting and I still don't feel well.

Charlie doesn't say a word but comes up to Willie and gives him a hug. Willie responds and wipes a tear from his eye. He leaves and Charlie watches him go. He wipes a tear from his eye and leaves.

<u>*End of Scene One.*</u>

Scene Two: *Several months later. Deidre enters, sits on a park bench and pulls out a book from her case. She is well dressed and attractive. Willie enters, dressed casually, and walks with a cane and a slight limp. She rises, gives him a hug and they both sit.*

DEIDRE
You made it. I wasn't sure you would.

WILLIE
It's good to get out. It's been a long time. How've you been?

DEIDRE
Pas mal. Could be better.

WILLIE
Quel dommage. I need to speak French, in case I get there one day.

DEIDRE
Good. Keep it up. It's a beautiful language.

WILLIE
You look terrific.

DEIDRE
Thanks. And you're looking much better.

WILLIE
A lot of people say that. Considering how bad I was.

DEIDRE
I've lost track. It's been several years, hasn't it?

WILLIE
A few. It's great to see you again.

DEIDRE
As I remember, you'd had radiation for bladder cancer, right?

WILLIE
Yep. The radiation caused proctitis, but that was just the start.

DEIDRE
What do you mean?

WILLIE
It turned out to be a massive abscess they'd overlooked. Lost forty-five pounds. I was about to go septic, they said.

DEIDRE
Septic? That's poisonous, isn't it?

WILLIE
It sure is. But I was lucky. They got it in time. I almost bought it.

DEIDRE
To tell you the truth, when I saw you, I wasn't sure you'd make it.

WILLIE
I'm pretty hard to kill.

DEIDRE
Don't joke, Willie. Tell me the truth. Were you ever in doubt?

WILLIE
Of course. When everyone around you has that look, expecting you to go, how can you not have doubts? In fact, sometimes I thought people were thinking 'get on with it.'

DEIDRE
I was pretty sick from chemo but I never felt that way.

WILLIE
When one doctor after another gives up, walks away, throws in the towel, it's pretty hard to be positive. When people turn away, don't know what to say, steer clear, you feel pretty much alone.

DEIDRE
The doctors missed it, didn't they?

WILLIE

Many did. They missed a lot. They didn't look hard enough. They gave up. I feel doctors want to help with success but walk away from failure, don't want to be involved if they can't chalk up a win.

DEIDRE

Don't be so bitter.

WILLIE

I'm not bitter, just observant.

DEIDRE

Some doctors may be like that, Willie, but most of them are good and want to help the best they can.

WILLIE

I'm glad you've had those experiences. And then there's always more.

DEIDRE

What do you mean? More what? Doctors? Tests?

WILLIE

More they didn't tell you. More they didn't look for, didn't find.

DEIDRE

Are you alright? Something wrong?

WILLIE

I didn't want to talk about my health. I haven't seen you for years.

DEIDRE

It's alright. You can talk about it. What is it?

WILLIE

Now it's my lungs.

DEIDRE

Oh, hell. What's wrong?

WILLIE

Some sort of infection. I'm going to see the doc to learn what he and the others have to say.

DEIDRE

Have they done any tests?

WILLIE

Lots. They've sent the results even to specialists across the country.

DEIDRE

I hope it's not too serious.

WILLIE

We'll see. But let's talk about happier times. Something upbeat.

DEIDRE

I'll try. Remember when we met years ago? They were talking about Warren Buffett while we waited for our blood draw.

WILLIE

We were in select company. He was having radiation treatment at the same time as many of us.

DEIDRE

We think we're alone, don't we? But there's a special bond between those that go through chemo or radiation or surgery or whatever. We understand each other.

WILLIE

And to know even Buffett has gone through it. That brought some smiles to those sitting with us.

DEIDRE

Shall we go for coffee?

WILLIE

Wait just a few minutes. Charlie might join us. I haven't seen him for months. Did I mention him before?

DEIDRE
Charlie? *(Startled.)* No. I don't think I've ever met him. How do you know him?

WILLIE
He's an old friend from the theatre. I'd like you to meet him. You two seem to have so much in common.

CHARLIE
(Charlie enters. They stand.) Am I late? *(Gives Willie a brief hug.)*

WILLIE
You're fine. We just got here. *(To Deidre.)* This is Charlie.

Charlie sees Deidre and pulls back, startled. She tries to stay calm.

CHARLIE
(Shakes her hand.) Glad to meet you. Willie's mentioned you before.

DEIDRE
(She holds his handshake for a moment.) Something good I hope.

CHARLIE
(He holds her hand then steps back.) Nothing but the highest praise.

WILLIE
(To Charlie.) Well? How is Todd?

CHARLIE
He passed away several weeks ago. *(Wipes away a tear, his voice quavers.)* He'd been out of it for several days. I just held his hand. He seemed to know I was there, heard my voice, squeezed my hand.

WILLIE
I'm sorry. *(To Deidre.)* He's from the theatre. Had colon cancer.

CHARLIE
You'd never see him on stage but he made it all work. Always calm. Never panicked as opening night got closer and it all seemed a disaster. But it always came together.

WILLIE

I'm going to leave you two. I want to check with the doctor's office about my latest test results. Meet you above for coffee. *(He leaves.)*

CHARLIE

Alright. *(To Willie as he goes. Turns to Deidre.)* He kept talking about you. I didn't believe it could be you.

DEIDRE

(She sits and he joins her.) He mentioned your name and said we were so alike. I could hardly breathe.

CHARLIE

(Their hands touch and she grasps his.) Willie said he met you in a Master Gardener class. You've a green thumb?

DEIDRE

Not really. We were partners. We had fun. That was long ago. Then we met again running alongside each other in a marathon, but we didn't talk much. It was mile twenty.

CHARLIE

I can understand that.

DEIDRE

We met again waiting for a blood draw. Long wait. We were sitting next to each other, listening to people sharing their experiences. One woman had radiation to cure one cancer, which caused another.

CHARLIE

What types of cancer?

DEIDRE

I'm not sure. She may have had breast cancer and then lung cancer or the other way around. I can't remember.

CHARLIE

I've heard of that for radiation in the lower GI system. Cure one and cause another.

DEIDRE
A man next to her said he'd had prostate cancer then colon cancer, as I remember.

CHARLIE
So, then you and Willie started talking?

DEIDRE
Yes. We talked about ourselves, then somehow got into politics.

CHARLIE
Dangerous.

DEIDRE
You're right. We soon realized we had different views.

CHARLIE
About what?

DEIDRE
Remember this was years ago when we first met. He didn't seem to like the idea of a woman as president.

CHARLIE
He must've been happy when we didn't get our first one.

DEIDRE
Yes, but I don't think he liked the idea of our first black president either. I'm not sure.

CHARLIE
Well, we got one and I think he's terrific. Do you know who Willie did like?

DEIDRE
I don't think he liked any of them.

CHARLIE
He's in good company then. Lots of people feel that way.

DEIDRE

It's alright to want good honest politicians. What I don't understand is the hatred. It's vicious.

CHARLIE

It's true. We've lots of it out there, don't we? Where's it come from?

DEIDRE

It's taught. From parents, friends, religious leaders. Fueled by fear and ignorance.

CHARLIE

I'm not so sure. I think it's innate.

DEIDRE

What do you mean?

CHARLIE

They call it implicit bias. Almost nobody would admit to being prejudiced. In fact, most of us honestly believe that we aren't.

DEIDRE

And we are?

CHARLIE

Yes, and we bend over backward to show we're not.

DEIDRE

You mean "Some of my best friends are.. My attorney is."?

CHARLIE

Yes. Fortunately, most people don't act on their biases.

DEIDRE

Even judges that are required to be fair? They're biased?

CHARLIE

Even judges.

DEIDRE

So how do you get to hatred from there?

CHARLIE

They become bigots. Racists, misogynists, coming out of the woods. It becomes acceptable.

DEIDRE

Reinforced by people in very high positions of authority?

CHARLIE

And then by others with their views. And slanted news. Hatred and mob violence become alright. It's frightening.

DEIDRE

It's sad, Charlie. And saddest of all: it's irrational. You can't reason with such deep fear and hatred.

CHARLIE

I just hope that education replaces fear and understanding replaces hatred.

DEIDRE

You know Willie pretty well. Which way does he lean with his views?

CHARLIE

Not sure. We talk about theatre: plays, acting, directing, writing, people, ideas, and lots of memories.

DEIDRE

No idea about his politics?

CHARLIE

He's full of humanity, humor, love of land, and people. You'll never find a better friend. That's enough for me.

DEIDRE

What do you mean by better friend?

CHARLIE
If you need someone to play a part, he'll step in. If you need someone to direct your play, he'll step in. If you need someone to talk to, to cheer you up, someone to encourage you, he'll be there. He'd give you the shirt off his back.

DEIDRE
That's a true friend.

CHARLIE
He writes heart-warming humorous plays and encourages many of us to do the same. He's the most supportive and positive and helpful person I've ever met. His politics are about people, helping people.

DEIDRE
I know you have a lot of passion but I never heard you speak like this before.

CHARLIE
Willie and I are writers and observers of people. That's our job.

DEIDRE
I understand.

CHARLIE
I'll tell you this: many of the people involved with politics are adept at using people. Willie is the exact opposite of this. He cares about people, and is generous with his time and talent.

DEIDRE
He knows us pretty well, and brought us back together, hasn't he?

CHARLIE
That he did. *(Touches her hand again.)* What about you? Who do you like in the political arena?

DEIDRE
I think she'd be one of the best presidents we've ever had.

CHARLIE
We may never know.

DEIDRE
You'll see many more elections, so stop talking like that. Tell me about your political preferences.

CHARLIE
I can tell you who I don't like. That semi-illiterate charlatan.

DEIDRE
Name calling doesn't help, Charlie.

CHARLIE
You're right. Anger's not healthy.

DEIDRE
Then tell me who you like.

CHARLIE
I started out liking the finger-waving one-issue guy.

DEIDRE
Hmmm. There you go again.

CHARLIE
I don't like the sexist part, but he has good ideas, ideas we need.

DEIDRE
(A bit sharp.) And where do they come from?

CHARLIE
Let's not argue, Deidre.

DEIDRE
We haven't yet, but I think we should stay away from politics.

CHARLIE
I agree. Sex, religion, and politics.

DEIDRE

Well, it's alright to talk about sex.

CHARLIE

You haven't changed a bit. You said you were having a blood draw? Cancer?

DEIDRE

That was years ago. Breast cancer, stage one. I'm lucky. In remission now.

CHARLIE

We're all in remission. Any of us could get anything anytime so we're all in remission.

DEIDRE

(She stares at him intently.) Why are you so negative?

CHARLIE

I'm not. Just a bit philosophical.

DEIDRE

What did you have?

CHARLIE

Prostate.

DEIDRE

Is it in remission also?

CHARLIE

Not quite. Comes back slowly.

DEIDRE

How've you been all these years? It's been a long time. Are you married?

CHARLIE

I was.

DEIDRE
But not now?

CHARLIE
Lost my wife.

DEIDRE
How?

CHARLIE
She died.

DEIDRE
You're so casual about it.

CHARLIE
I'm sorry. Didn't mean to be. I didn't think you'd be interested.

DEIDRE
(She looks down hiding her hurt feelings.) I'm sorry I intruded.

CHARLIE
You didn't. I was rude. It's just something I'd rather not talk about.

DEIDRE
Kids?

CHARLIE
A son.

DEIDRE
Any grandkids?

CHARLIE
(Brightens up.) There's nothing more enjoyable than spending time with grandchildren. I adore grandchildren.

Two women walk by slowly, arguing as they go.

FIRST WOMAN
He's won most of the primaries and the nomination.

SECOND WOMAN
Personal attacks on primary opponents, no substance, no ideas, lie after lie every day, that wins, I guess. What a disgrace. We have such idiots in the GOP.

FIRST WOMAN
Now wait a minute. He's a good businessman. Maybe we need someone like that for a change. Throw the bums out.

SECOND WOMAN
What bums? Are you talking about the congress? The GOP senators and representatives?

FIRST WOMAN
All of them. Just get rid of all of them. Drain the swamp.

SECOND WOMAN
How're you going to do that? What're you talking about? At least he won't win the election.

FIRST WOMAN
Don't be so sure of that. He's fooled a lot of people so far.

Deidre and Charlie watch them leave. One of them drops a handkerchief but Charlie and Deidre just look at it.

DEIDRE
At least one of them has her head on straight.

CHARLIE
Yes, but I'm afraid there may be a lot more like the other one.

DEIDRE
We have to hope there are more of the first one, don't we?

CHARLIE
Yes. I'm usually optimistic but this time is a great test for all of us.

The two women return. One of them picks up the handkerchief.

SECOND WOMAN
So, what's wrong with him? He never gets out, he just sits at home, never votes. He's just a useless lump.

FIRST WOMAN
Now wait a minute. He's not that bad. He cooks now and then.

SECOND WOMAN
How often?

FIRST WOMAN
(Thinks.) Maybe once a month.

SECOND WOMAN
See what I mean. What kind of a husband is that? Drain the swamp. Dump him.

The two women disappear, mumbling.

CHARLIE
Speaking of husbands, what about you? Married?

DEIDRE
I met Peter a few years ago. But it was short-lived. He died of brain cancer not too long ago.

CHARLIE
Sorry. *(He moves closer to her but catches himself.)*

DEIDRE
It's alright. We had a good life. Made the best of it. He went quickly.

CHARLIE
You haven't changed much. Still as beautiful as ever.

DEIDRE
You're looking pretty good too. I'll never forget…*(Stops.)*

CHARLIE
Forget what?

DEIDRE
Our last time.

CHARLIE
I didn't want to let go of you.

DEIDRE
We were under that waterfall. Clinging to each other. You held me so tightly. I could hardly breathe.

CHARLIE
I felt as if we were one.

DEIDRE
We merged together, Charlie. I couldn't tell where you ended and I began. It was magical.

They move together as they remember. They put their arms around each other.

CHARLIE
I knew we might not see each other again.

DEIDRE
But we have, Charlie. We have. It's wonderful.

CHARLIE
The other reason I held you so tightly was that it was cold.

DEIDRE
(Laughs.) As I remember it didn't seem to bother you. You were really turned on. It was exciting.

CHARLIE
You turned me on.

DEIDRE

I'll never forget. Never.

CHARLIE

(They separate, still holding hands.) I remember the first time.

DEIDRE

What first time?

CHARLIE

When we climbed that mountain in the summertime. And stayed over because of the weather.

DEIDRE

(Frowns.) Nothing happened then.

CHARLIE

But you didn't know that. You thought you were pregnant. That's what your friend said.

DEIDRE

I was so innocent. I had no idea. We curled up all night together to stay warm.

CHARLIE

With our clothes on.

DEIDRE

I didn't know any better, Charlie. I lead a very sheltered life.

CHARLIE

I built a roaring fire. But it was still cold.

Long awkward pause. Neither knows what to say.

DEIDRE

It was a mistake.

CHARLIE

What was?

DEIDRE
Leaving you. But we were so young. I wasn't ready.

CHARLIE
Then it wasn't a mistake, was it?

DEIDRE
I was too young to appreciate you. I had to live a little.

CHARLIE
Did you?

DEIDRE
(Takes a deep breath.) To be honest, Charlie, I fled. I fled from you, from love, the intensity of our relationship.

CHARLIE
Where'd you go? You often talked about wanting to go to Rome.

DEIDRE
E vero. It's true. I always wanted to see Rome. It was fantastic. I was sitting near Fontana di Trevi one day, the water trickling down, and I thought of you and the waterfall. I've thought of you often since.

CHARLIE
I lived there for a few years. A beautiful city. A beautiful country. Look up, not down, as the saying goes.

DEIDRE
While I was in Rome, I became friends with a woman, older, very worldly. She was married to an Italian, an Englishman, an American, and had many lovers which she talked about often. She said quietly once that Americans were the best lovers. I asked why.

CHARLIE
And what did she say?

DEIDRE

She said the Italians were mama's boys, the English were uptight, but the Americans were gentle and considerate and treated her like a woman. Then I thought of you, Charlie.

CHARLIE

The waterfall again?

DEIDRE

No, before that. I thought of some of our good times back here in the city. Remember that restaurant that served crepes? We loved going there. We sat listening to very private conversations. A mother and daughter, a couple breaking up, lots of drama.

CHARLIE

I felt we were really intruding into some very personal stuff.

DEIDRE

It wasn't our fault. They chose to have that discussion in the restaurant. But I agree. It's pretty personal.

CHARLIE

In Rome. Any Italian lovers? Or English?

DEIDRE

(She giggles.) Stop it, Charlie. You were my American lover. That was enough. I just wanted to travel, to live, to meet people. So, I left Rome, went to Paris first, then London.

CHARLIE

What did you do to support yourself?

DEIDRE

I had a couple of jobs doing translations. I don't know if you remember but I'd studied Italian and French.

CHARLIE

Yes, I remember you talking to waiters in French and Italian restaurants here in the city.

DEIDRE

Do you know they didn't know the language here? Only a bit in one of the Italian restaurants.

CHARLIE

How long were you in Europe?

DEIDRE

Several years. I lived frugally in Rome and Paris, but London was expensive. Then I came home.

CHARLIE

Is that where you met Peter? Over there?

DEIDRE

No, much later, after I returned. I had enough adventure and decided to go back to business school. I'd inherited money, bought a farm and raised animals and produce. That's when I met Peter.

CHARLIE

On the farm?

DEIDRE

He managed a large farm nearby and helped me get started, advising me in buying animals. We became good friends, then decided to live together. He was a business partner as much as anything.

CHARLIE

Where was the farm?

DEIDRE

Do you know where Bodega Bay is?

CHARLIE

Are you kidding? After Hitchcock made The Birds, who doesn't?

DEIDRE

Well, it was between Petaluma and Bodega. Beautiful farming country.

CHARLIE

I know the country well. Hot and sometimes very windy. *(He can hardly say it.)* Any kids?

DEIDRE

(She falters. Almost reduced to tears.) No. It was too late for that.

CHARLIE

And then? Your farm? You and Peter?

DEIDRE

That's when I got breast cancer. It took a lot out of me. And Peter. We were never the same after that.

CHARLIE

(Pensive.) Cancer takes a lot out of everyone, doesn't it?

DEIDRE

It was much harder on Peter than it was on me.

CHARLIE

It's a helpless feeling to be close to someone and not be able to help.

DEIDRE

Charlie, I've thought of you many times, more than you can imagine.

CHARLIE

I've often wondered where you went, what you were doing, were you happy, if I'd ever see you again.

DEIDRE

Now you know that I travelled a lot. I've been pretty happy, I guess. And here we are.

CHARLIE

When you were in Rome, did you go to the Vatican Museum?

DEIDRE

Often.

CHARLIE

I was lucky. One day I was in the Sistine Chapel and there were only a few people there. I lay on my back and looked up at the ceiling. Extraordinary. I could see Michelangelo's struggle with scale and proportion, the difference between the early part, and the later part.

DEIDRE

It was always jammed when I was there. Did you ever get to the Louvre in Paris?

CHARLIE

Several times. But I love Rome the most. Art is everywhere: in the churches, the fountains, wherever you go.

DEIDRE

Especially in the churches. Every church.

CHARLIE

I remember a Caravaggio I saw in a church off Piazza Navona.

DEIDRE

I went there too, but I heard that the Italians learned to promote and market their treasures. It's changed, hasn't it?

CHARLIE

Alas, it has. Everyone knows where all the artworks are now.

DEIDRE

You can't just go quickly into an empty church, turn a light on, and gaze without interruption. Now you have to stand in line to see that beautiful Caravaggio. His chiaroscuro technique. The light contrast is extraordinary.

CHARLIE

The Italians are becoming more like the British.

DEIDRE

I had dinner in a small ristorante near Piazza Navona. Down a side street. You would've loved it.

CHARLIE

I know the one you mean. The end toward the river. Out and to the left. I went there a few times.

DEIDRE

Remember that tiny restaurant we went to in the city when we met?

CHARLIE

Yes. It was intimate.

DEIDRE

We held hands and looked at each other. I didn't see anyone else.

CHARLIE

I was oblivious of anything or anyone except you.

DEIDRE

I wish you'd been with me in that little ristorante off Piazza Navona.

CHARLIE

I wish that too.

DEIDRE

Or another one I loved near the Pantheon. One day it started to rain and I dashed into the Pantheon. It was glorious. The rain drifted down through the opening at the top in the center, shimmering in the sunlight above. The water ran down to the edges of the circular floor. I imagined standing there holding your hand.

CHARLIE

Were you lonely in Rome?

DEIDRE

(Wipes away a tear.) Terribly. When the rain stopped, I went to a ristorante up a side street. I was crying. You would never see an Italian woman eating alone. The Italians are a warm loving sociable people. Eating out is a major social event, much more than just eating. So, there I was, a woman eating alone, and weeping.

He puts his hand on her shoulder. She puts her hand on his.

CHARLIE
That's considered a major crime in Rome, a woman eating alone. *(She tries to smile through her tears.)* Did you know that the two best places to have coffee in Rome were both near the Pantheon?

She smiles broadly and puts her arm around him.

DEIDRE
I wish we could have done some of those things together. Willie was right. We had so much in common.

CHARLIE
Have much in common. Speaking of coffee and Willie, we'd better get on up there to meet him.

They leave.

<u>End of Scene Two.</u>

Scene Three*: In a corner of the local coffee shop. Willie sits sipping a coffee and reading a paper and occasionally nods to someone he knows. He looks at his watch, gets up and leaves with his coffee and paper still on the table. A moment later Deidre and Charlie enter.*

WAITRESS
(She recognizes Charlie. She points to Willie's table.) He just left but it looks as if he's coming back.

They sit at his table and settle in.

DEIDRE
(To waitress.) Due cappuccini.

CHARLIE
E due cornetti, per favore.

They look at each other and start laughing uproariously. She reaches out to touch him and moves closer.

WAITRESS
What'd you say?

DEIDRE
(Regains composure.) Two coffees please. A latte.

CHARLIE
And a double mocha. *(Looks at Deidre.)* And two muffins. One bran.

DEIDRE
And a morning glory.

WAITRESS
(Just stands there.) A what?

CHARLIE
(Sotto voce.) That's a flower.

DEIDRE
(Rattled.) Good morning muffin.

Waitress walks away shaking head. They look at each other giggling.

CHARLIE
I remember a little café in Trastevere. Across the piazza from the Basilica di Santa Maria.

DEIDRE
Exactly. I'd sit there, sipping a cappuccino in the sun. I could look across at the Madonna and Child at the top of the campanile. There were so many people sitting on the steps of the fountain.

CHARLIE
It's believed to be the oldest fountain in Rome.

DEIDRE
I'm sure the people there didn't know that, but would've enjoyed it even more if they did.

CHARLIE
It's a very beautiful fountain.

DEIDRE
When it was very hot I went inside to the coolness of the church.

CHARLIE
It's one of the oldest churches in Rome, dating back to the early part of the third century.

DEIDRE
(She tickles him.) Oh, Charlie.

CHARLIE
Did you know the columns came from the Terme di Caracalla?

DEIDRE
And did you see the Cavallini?

CHARLIE
Yes. Spanning the apse above the altar.

DEIDRE

Did you know you sound like a travel guide? It was the beginning of movement in art, after the static form of Byzantine art, symbolic and anti-naturalistic, the beginning of Roman naturalism.

CHARLIE

(He roars with laughter. She smiles.) And you sound like an art lecturer. Touché! Alright, you win. I gather you also went to Santa Cecilia in Trastevere to see his masterwork of Roman naturalism?

DEIDRE

I lived in Trastevere. Did I mention that? I spent many days there.

CHARLIE

That makes sense. It's a short distance to Piazza Navona and the Pantheon from there and you said you were very lonely. Deidre, I.. *(He falters, unable to express his feelings.)*

DEIDRE

You can't imagine how lonely I was. Oh Charlie, I wish we could go there together. To see Caravaggios and Cavallinis in the churches, to stroll through the little streets together, to have cappuccinni e cornetti in charming cafes, and to dine together in the late warm summer evenings, listening to the music of Rome.

They are interrupted by the waitress who brings two muffins.

CHARLIE

(To waitress.) The man that left before we got here. Did he say anything about where he was going?

WAITRESS

Just mumbled something. I think he said "they must know by now".

DEIDRE

He must have been talking about the blood tests. He said he wanted to check with the doctor's office about them.

CHARLIE
(To waitress.) Did he say anything about when he would return?

WAITRESS
Nope. He just left. *(She leaves.)*

DEIDRE
He's been really worried about an infection in his lungs.

CHARLIE
(Starts to get up.) I have a terrible feeling. I should go find him.

DEIDRE
(Puts her hand on his shoulder to stop him.) You don't know, Charlie. Wait until he comes back.

CHARLIE
(Hesitates, focuses on Deidre.) I just have an awful premonition.

DEIDRE
Don't jump to conclusions. Wait a minute. He'll be back soon.

CHARLIE
(Relaxes just a bit.) Did you ever get to see Terme di Caracalla?

DEIDRE
It's outside the city but I got there once. The mosaics were still there. Beautiful. I can imagine the social life there.

CHARLIE
The social life in the frigidarium, tepidarium, or caldarium?

DEIDRE
You mean the frigidarium like the waterfall? Couldn't compare.

CHARLIE
So, their social life was in the tepidarium and caldarium?

DEIDRE
I think I would have preferred the tepidarium.

CHARLIE
You should see it at night in the summer when they have opera on the southwest side where the caldarium was.

DEIDRE
You mean the way it was in the Three Tenors?

CHARLIE
Yes. I saw Aida and Turandot there. Elephants and all. But Turandot is my favorite opera.

DEIDRE
(Wistfully. She turns away.) It must have been lovely.

CHARLIE
It was very special for me. *(He's not sure what to say.)* Did you ever see the underground Mithraic temple there?

DEIDRE
I heard about it but never went there. What did it look like?

CHARLIE
Stark and simple. It was small, stone benches on the side, and an area in the middle where they sacrificed the bull.

DEIDRE
Remember that little nightclub where we danced away the night?

CHARLIE
Vividly.

DEIDRE
It overlooked the harbor, the still water glittering in the moonlight.

CHARLIE
I remember we asked the band to play our favorite song.

DEIDRE
Just like Casablanca. As Time Goes By.

A flashback. The lights fade on the current scene and come up on a past scene. The lights are low and music plays softly. Charlie and Deidre dance closely together to As Time Goes By. *He sings.*

CHARLIE
You must remember this. A kiss is just a kiss. A sigh is just a sigh.

DEIDRE
(She joins in.) The fundamental things apply. As time goes by.

CHARLIE
(Sings.) And when two lovers woo, they still say, "I love you." On that you can rely.

DEIDRE
(Sings.) No matter what the future brings. As time goes by.

They dance silently together. The music fades. The lights come up.

CHARLIE
Time is going by, isn't it?

DEIDRE
You mean now? Waiting for Willie?

CHARLIE
No, what Todd told me. Make every day count. We still have time.

DEIDRE
Charlie, do you really think so?

CHARLIE
I learned during the darkest of days, that whilst I live and breathe, I will make the best of my time. "It is not for us to decide how much time we have. All we have to decide is what to do with the time that is given us."

DEIDRE
Gandalf? *(She smiles, then puts her head down.)* Oh, I don't know.

CHARLIE

I look forward to getting up every morning, doing something useful, and I care. I wasn't the first to say that but it is my motto. I do care, about the planet, about the people on it, and especially about you. I care very much about you.

DEIDRE

Charlie, there's something I haven't told you.

They are interrupted and startled by Willie walking in, head down, shaking his head, dazed and confused. Charlie jumps up and tries to help him to sit but Willie doesn't want to sit.

DEIDRE

What is it, Willie? What's wrong?

WILLIE

They told me the results. It's worse than they thought. I'm meeting the doctor for the details.

He looks around and starts walking unsteadily the wrong way, and then finally out the door he came in. Charlie follows him and takes him by the arm to steady him.

CHARLIE

I'm with you, Willie. I'll go with you.

Deidre puts her hands to her eyes, puts her head down on the table, and sobs.

<u>End of Scene Three.</u>

<u>End of Act One.</u>

ACT TWO

Scene One: *The coffee shop, several months later. Early in the day. Deidre reads. The waitress has a coffee and a croissant in her hand.*

WAITRESS
No cornetto to go with your cappuccino. Would a croissant do?

DEIDRE
(She smiles and nods.) That'd be lovely. J'adore les croissants.

The waitress smiles, leaves the croissant as Charlie enters.

CHARLIE
(To waitress.) Cappuccino e cornetto, per favore. *(Sits.)*

WAITRESS
Cappuccino e croissant?

CHARLIE
Va bene, Grazie. Merci.

WAITRESS
Prego. De rien. *(She leaves.)*

CHARLIE
I'm glad you're back. You disappeared after we heard about Willie.

DEIDRE
I'm sorry, Charlie, for leaving so suddenly without telling you.

CHARLIE
I was worried until I got the letter. You've been gone three months.

DEIDRE
I had some business to take care of. It took some time, Charlie.

CHARLIE
When you called yesterday, I was so glad. Is everything alright?

He reaches out to hold her hand. She responds gently.

DEIDRE
Everything's fine. How is Willie doing?

CHARLIE
He's in good spirits.

DEIDRE
Are they absolutely sure? It's so final, stage four lung cancer.

CHARLIE
They're sure. I talked to him on the phone. He said he'd join us.

DEIDRE
He's been through so much.

CHARLIE
He's at peace. He's accepted the decision.

DEIDRE
Is the prognosis final?

CHARLIE
Nothing's ever final, but several doctors have concurred. I don't mean to intrude, but can I help?

DEIDRE
It's alright. Some family business to straighten out. I'm just tired.

CHARLIE
Your letter said something about a farm.

DEIDRE
In California. Remember saying how hot and windy it is there?

CHARLIE
The wind can be ferocious.

DEIDRE
Well, it was just plain hot. The farmhouse isn't air conditioned.

CHARLIE

I'm glad you're back. Three months is a long time. I've missed you.

DEIDRE

(They hold hands more strongly.) I've missed you too.

CHARLIE

Before you left you said there was something you hadn't told me? We were interrupted by Willie. What was it?

DEIDRE

You remembered all this time? It's about Rome. Long ago.

CHARLIE

What about Rome?

DEIDRE

I was very lonely, and I wanted so much to call you. Then a friend told me she heard you were getting married.

CHARLIE

You were going to call me? Why?

DEIDRE

It was foolish of me I guess. I hoped you'd join me for a few days.

CHARLIE

You're serious? I thought you said you fled, to get away.

DEIDRE

I also said it was a mistake.

CHARLIE

If you'd called, I would've gone in a minute.

DEIDRE

But you were getting married.

CHARLIE

That didn't happen.

DEIDRE
What do you mean?

Waitress brings his cappuccino and his croissant.

CHARLIE
Grazie mille.

WAITRESS
Prego.

CHARLIE
(She leaves. To Deidre.) I mean that I was engaged but I called it off.

Willie walks in with a cane. They stand up and each gives him a hug.

DEIDRE
This isn't fair, Willie.

Waitress comes over.

WILLIE
Weak herbal tea. *(She leaves.)* I've had a good life. I can't complain.

DEIDRE
Are you in a lot of pain?

WILLIE
(Nods yes.) But I've got my meds. And my other pills.

DEIDRE
What pills?

WILLIE
It's called "Death with Dignity". Needed signatures of two doctors.

DEIDRE
So, when you can't stand the pain anymore, you take the pills? At home?

WILLIE
That's the idea. The tumor's already breaking through my ribs.

DEIDRE
Oh, Willie. *(Tears start.)*

WILLIE
It's alright. Hospice helps me but they won't be there at pill time.

Starts to choke up but controls it. Drops his voice, lowers his head.

DEIDRE
You can't be alone for this.

WILLIE
I have a son that lives close by. He'll be there when the time comes.

CHARLIE
Willie, I hope it doesn't come to that. I'm praying for a miracle.

WILLIE
Thanks for that, but I'm afraid there won't be any miracle this time.

Reality sinks in. Waitress brings his tea. He sips it but it's too hot.

CHARLIE
No one else there besides your son?

WILLIE
I've been wanting to ask if you'd be there with me.

CHARLIE
Of course. You've always been there for others. I'd be honored.

WILLIE
I won't ask you, Deidre. You told me once you don't like funerals.

DEIDRE
This isn't a funeral. If you want me, I'll be there.

WILLIE

Alright guys. Let's get off this. I'm still here. Tell me about Rome.

Two women enter to get coffee, in the middle of an argument.

FIRST WOMAN

Don't blame me.

SECOND WOMAN

I do blame you, and three million other cowards.

FIRST WOMAN

I didn't vote for him.

SECOND WOMAN

But you didn't vote for her and that's the same thing.

FIRST WOMAN

I can't help it he was elected.

SECOND WOMAN

Yes, you can. What I hate is you don't take responsibility for your actions. I call you the "alt-one percent". Not even a percent, not half of one. By not voting you're responsible for the crook we now have.

FIRST WOMAN

I have a right to not vote for her.

SECOND WOMAN

And you have the right and privilege to take responsibility for his election. You and several other million cowards.

WILLIE

Damn right! *(Charges.)* You're a damn coward. Step up. Be a man.

CHARLIE

(He restrains him from hitting her.) Easy, Willie. Take it easy.

DEIDRE

It's a woman, Willie.

The women run out.

WILLIE

She knows what I mean.

CHARLIE

Calm down, Willie. It won't do any good to get so excited.

WILLIE

People like that make me mad. They don't take responsibility. Somebody else's problem. Don't blame me. Bullshit.

DEIDRE

(Puts her hand on his shoulder.) You need to calm down Willie.

WILLIE

(He sits.) I'm calm now. Where were we?

CHARLIE

You wanted us to tell you about Rome.

WILLIE

Yes, tell me about it and other faraway places. I've always wanted to go to Europe. Let me dream a bit.

CHARLIE

Let's help you dream then. Any food or drinks to avoid?

WILLIE

Not yet. As far as I know food and drink don't go through the lungs.

CHARLIE

That's the attitude.

DEIDRE

Here goes. The best chocolates in Rome, near the two best coffee shops, are on a side street near the Pantheon.

CHARLIE

All sorts of fabulous chocolates.

WILLIE
Sounds wonderful. I can taste them in my mind.

DEIDRE
And pasta. There are so many kinds of delicious pastas, in restaurants and grocery stores.

CHARLIE
My favorite was penne all' arrabbiata. I tried it in many restaurants throughout Rome, just to compare.

DEIDRE
And your conclusion?

CHARLIE
Always different, always good.

WILLIE
You can't get off that easily. Which restaurant had the best?

CHARLIE
(Pretends to think.) Alright. Down a side street near the Vatican. Roberto's, I think it was called.

DEIDRE
Do you like cheese, Willie?

WILLIE
I love it, especially soft and creamy cheese.

DEIDRE
You'd love the gorgonzola in Rome. I'd linger over my gorgonzola at the end of a meal, savoring it.

WILLIE
Where was this?

DEIDRE
I remember sitting at a small restaurant off of Piazza Navona, looking out at Bernini's Fontana del Quattro Fiumi.

WILLIE

(Eyes closed.) I can picture myself doing the same, with some strong Italian red wine, maybe Brunello or Barolo.

CHARLIE

Way to go, Willie! You're getting pretty good at dreaming.

DEIDRE

You've beat me on that one, Willie.

CHARLIE

And now, I'll take you to southern France. You go down the hill to the shore of the Mediterranean, to a little town called Bouziques on the Etang de Thau and buy a few dozen huitres de Bouziques.

WILLIE

When is this?

CHARLIE

You go between September and April, months with an R. The French love oysters, especially at New Year's.

DEIDRE

You just went to get the oysters. Now what? You digress.

CHARLIE

Alright. Alright. You buy a bottle of good champagne and share it and the oysters with friends, *(looks at Deidre.)* Or a special friend.

WILLIE

I can almost taste the oysters.

DEIDRE

Now describe the taste, Charlie. What's it like?

CHARLIE

It's delicious. Slide the oyster into your mouth. It's like, it's like.

DEIDRE

Like sex?

CHARLIE

That's it. You've got it.

WILLIE

This sounds better all the time.

There's a long silence, finally broken by Charlie.

CHARLIE

You can find many types of fish on the shore of the Med. There're over 700 kinds. Mullet, seabass, turbot, sole.

DEIDRE

Even shark.

CHARLIE

Yes, even shark. Once I was sitting in a restaurant with a friend, outside in the warm air, only thirty feet from the Med. We were served a wonderful platter of fish.

DEIDRE

Even the Great White shark is in the Mediterranean.

CHARLIE

Not on the platter. Bouillabaisse can have rascasse, grondin, conger, dorade, turbot, lotte, mullet, merian, moules…

DEIDRE

Even shark.

WILLIE

Alright, guys, enough! I'll stay with oysters and champagne and get to the fish some other time.

Willie starts to rise, struggling to stand up.

DEIDRE

You have to leave?

WILLIE

I'm getting tired. I don't want to overdo it.

DEIDRE

We understand.

They get up and give Willie another hug, and he walks slowly away.

CHARLIE

Do you think I talked too much?

DEIDRE

No, Charlie. That's part of your charm. Your enthusiasm. That is, most of the time. Do you think that helped? Give him something to dream about?

CHARLIE

Yes, he had a soft look. Until he got tired, probably of me.

DEIDRE

No, Charlie, it wasn't you. He winced. He left because of the pain.

CHARLIE

He didn't want to show the pain in front of us. Willie's a class act.

They sit down again. Each of them is thinking.

DEIDRE

You were telling me about breaking your engagement. Why?

CHARLIE

There were a couple of reasons I guess. When you left me, and fled to Europe, I was confused. I wasn't myself. They say one should never jump into another relationship so quickly. It's true.

DEIDRE

What do you mean?

CHARLIE

I was foolish, blind. I didn't see the signs, or just ignored them.

DEIDRE
You're not making sense, Charlie.

CHARLIE
She didn't tell the truth about many things. She was good at lying. In fact, I don't think she knew the difference between the truth and the lies. I really think she began to believe the lies were the truth.

DEIDRE
Like someone else we all know.

CHARLIE
The biggest lie in a way was not telling me something just before we were to be married.

DEIDRE
What was that?

CHARLIE
That she was already married to someone else.

DEIDRE
That's a pretty good reason to break your engagement.

CHARLIE
The truth is that I was still willing to go ahead and overlook that, once she got a divorce.

DEIDRE
And did you?

CHARLIE
There was a second reason: I realized you can't go marry someone when you're in love with someone else.

DEIDRE
(Silence as she moves closer to him and covers his hands with hers. They lean toward each other lingering on possibility of kissing, but hesitate.) Oh, Charlie, if I'd only known.

CHARLIE
And if I'd only known you really wanted me to join you. After I broke my engagement I wandered like a lost man.

DEIDRE
(She pulls back but continues to cover his hands with hers.) What's done is done, Charlie. There's no going back.

CHARLIE
We can go back by going forward, can't we?

DEIDRE
What about your family, your wife? You have a son and adorable grandchildren. We just can't go forward so easily.

CHARLIE
Deidre, I don't have any grandchildren. I'd love grandchildren and to adore them. That's what I meant before. As a matter of fact, I don't have any children either, not now.

DEIDRE
What are you saying? I don't understand.

CHARLIE
I had a son but I don't anymore.

DEIDRE
Charlie, you aren't making sense. My head is spinning.

CHARLIE
Some years after you left, I married someone and had a son. When he was three, they both died in an accident.

DEIDRE
My Lord, that's terrible.

CHARLIE
A drunken driver smashed into them on an overpass over a river. She lost control of her car and it went through a barrier and into the river. They both drowned. *(He starts to weep.)*

Deidre instinctively moves back closer to him, hesitates, then stands up and puts her arms around his shoulders, her head on his, and hugs him. He reaches up and puts his hands on hers. It is silent for a moment. It is quiet in the coffee shop but then a slight acquaintance of Charlie's sees him and comes over, intruding on their moment.

WOMAN/MAN
Hi, Charlie, how're you? Someone I don't know? *(To Deidre. Reaches out hand.)* Hello. I'm Priscilla.

CHARLIE
(Stands in front of Deidre. To the person.) We were just leaving.

He takes Deidre by the hand, heads for the exit, and the person trails after them.

WOMAN/MAN
But, Charlie, I'd love to meet your friend. *(They are gone. Drops her/his voice.)* Well, I'll be. Such manners.

End of Scene One.

Scene Two: *A park bench soon thereafter. Deidre and Charlie enter, still holding hands. They sit.*

DEIDRE
Charlie, you were mean but she deserved it. You know her well?

CHARLIE
A nosy neighbor type. I wasn't in the mood to be interrupted by her.

They are silent for a moment and return to their conversation.

DEIDRE
I understand. There's no worse time to intrude. Oh, I can't imagine how you must have felt. Tragic.

CHARLIE
It was a shock losing my wife, but she'd at least lived a little. But to lose my son that way. I've never recovered. It's left a deep wound.

DEIDRE
There's a saying: A man should never bury his son.

CHARLIE
Lord of the Rings. Yes, I know.

DEIDRE
Now I understand why you've never had grandchildren.

CHARLIE
It's strange. I always dreamed about having grandchildren one day. I saw others growing old and enjoying theirs. I was envious.

DEIDRE
But why didn't you marry again?

CHARLIE
It was enough to go through it twice. I didn't want to go through the shock and pain a third time. I had a job that allowed me to travel a lot, and even to live overseas, and I took every advantage of it.

DEIDRE
Such as traveling to Rome?

CHARLIE
Often. I remembered what you said about wanting to see Rome. I'll admit that I secretly wanted to run into you. I didn't know where you were or how to reach you but I dreamed about you.

DEIDRE
I've dreamed about you, Charlie. Many times.

CHARLIE
Finally, I gave up hope. I was lonely, as you were. I met some nice people, but I never got close to anyone. You were always there.

DEIDRE
You never would have found me.

CHARLIE
What did you say?

DEIDRE
When you travelled or lived there, you never would've found me.

CHARLIE
Why?

They're interrupted by two women having a loud argument.

FIRST WOMAN
She lost because she wasn't likeable.

SECOND WOMAN
He was likeable? Give me a break. She's more likeable than he, and still is. She got three million more votes in spite of foreign sabotage, complacency, voter suppression, and many supporting her primary opponent that didn't vote for her. It was stolen from her.

FIRST WOMAN

He's more presidential, and he was a successful businessman.

SECOND WOMAN

Successful? You call all those bankruptcies successful? Screwing working people. He's a crook, plain and simple. And he doesn't run things. Others always called the shots and still do. He's just a..

FIRST WOMAN

(Yelling loudly, interrupting.) You aren't being fair. He takes action quickly. He delivers what he promised.

SECOND WOMAN

(Yelling even more loudly.) You call impulsive reckless behavior taking action? Executive orders and proposals that screw the working people, especially those that mistakenly voted for him, you think that's what he promised? One day we'll find out he's guilty of treason, that he's being blackmailed, that..

FIRST WOMAN

(Interrupting, screaming as they exit.) Fox News says that's all lies. You don't know what you're talking about.

They disappear as Deidre and Charlie stare after them.

DEIDRE

How easily some people rationalize and forget the facts.

CHARLIE

It's called alternative facts.

DEIDRE

(She laughs,) Strange times we live in, Charlie.

CHARLIE

(They sit silently for a moment, again holding hands.) Before we were interrupted, you said that when I went to Europe, I wouldn't have found you. Why not?

DEIDRE

When I heard you were married, my hopes and dreams crumbled. I didn't want to come back here and I didn't have much money. I had an aunt that married an Italian and they lived in Trastevere.

CHARLIE

So, you did live in Trastevere?

DEIDRE

Yes, I was lucky. I'd planned to visit her anyway. Her husband helped me get a job translating.

CHARLIE

You stayed with them?

DEIDRE

For a while until I found my own place nearby. It was a struggle, but the job doing translating helped a bit.

CHARLIE

And what about Paris and London?

DEIDRE

I never went to London or saw much of Paris, Charlie. I did take a brief trip there to get a job translating French. They were flexible. I worked remotely and sent it back. It was difficult. Now it'd be easy.

CHARLIE

I don't understand. You were struggling. What about your parents?

DEIDRE

I can't remember what I told you. I'm having trouble remembering things. My parents from the Midwest weren't as understanding about my situation as my aunt and her Italian husband were.

CHARLIE

I see.

DEIDRE

Later we reconciled, just before they both died, a year apart. That's where my inheritance came from, for the farm.

CHARLIE

I'm beginning to understand. It's all fitting together.

DEIDRE

(Slowly.) Charlie, I said I fled to Europe to get away from you. That was true, but there was a bigger reason I didn't come back.

CHARLIE

(He leans forward, eyes wide open.) Bigger reason than leaving me?

DEIDRE

Yes. I was pregnant with our child.

CHARLIE

What? What did you say?

DEIDRE

(Very softly.) Charlie, you have a daughter.

CHARLIE

You mean that? We have a daughter? I really have a daughter?

DEIDRE

I found out for sure when I was in Italy. I didn't know what you would think. I was afraid, and then I saw you were going to get married. I just couldn't tell you then, I just couldn't call you.

CHARLIE

(He puts his arms around her.) Oh, my dear Deidre, you should have told me, you should have called me.

DEIDRE

(She snuggles into him.) I know, I know. When I said before I was lonely and wanted to call you, that was the real reason. I should've called but I just couldn't. What's done is done.

CHARLIE

Even if I was married I'd like to know we had a child. You should have known me better than that.

DEIDRE

I did Charlie. After she was born I realized that. I tried to reach you but you were gone. No one knew where.

CHARLIE

It's my fault. I was distraught. As I said before, I wandered, moved a lot. That's why you couldn't find me.

DEIDRE

I tried for weeks to find you and tell you. I finally gave up.

CHARLIE

As you said, what's done is done. *(They sit holding each other.)* You were all alone in Rome, expecting our child. What'd you do?

DEIDRE

(She takes a deep breath.) I decided to have our daughter there. What I said about my aunt was true. Besides the job translating, she and her husband helped me find a doctor.

CHARLIE

(He is quietly absorbing this reality.) What's our daughter's name?

DEIDRE

Carlotta. Named after you. When I was expecting Carlotta, I'd go to the piazza in Trastevere. I'd look across at Santa Maria just as I said. Sometimes I'd go across the river to Piazza Navona or the Pantheon.

CHARLIE

So that was true?

DEIDRE

All true. After she was born I'd take her to the same places.

CHARLIE

Oh Deidre, I wish I'd found you.

DEIDRE

As she grew older, we'd walk there together, but usually we'd go to a nearby park in our lovely neighborhood.

CHARLIE

I know what you mean. Just off the main tourist places, there're neighborhoods full of life, shops, piazzas, and friendly shopkeepers.

DEIDRE

I loved our neighborhood. Somehow, all the people understood and were sensitive to my situation and my sadness.

CHARLIE

(Softly and gently.) And the tears you mentioned? That was true?

DEIDRE

Charlie, so many tears and the deepest loneliness, you can't imagine.

CHARLIE

Yes, I can. Loneliness is something we can all understand. I only wish I'd known. *(He holds her tightly.)* How did you work and take care of her as well?

DEIDRE

I'd nurse her and go to work. Sometimes I'd take her with me, but if I couldn't I'd express milk. My aunt took care of her during the day.

CHARLIE

When she grew older, did you tell her she had a father?

DEIDRE

I didn't have to. She knew she was supposed to. Other kids did.

CHARLIE

Yes of course.

DEIDRE

Once she asked if she really had a father. "Where is he?", she said.

CHARLIE

And you told her she did and he loved her?

DEIDRE

Yes, Charlie. And I told her I didn't know where you were.

CHARLIE

Which was very true. I moved a lot.

DEIDRE

I would hear her crying herself asleep. I want my father, she would cry. It broke my heart.

CHARLIE

(Hugs her.) Oh, Deidre.

DEIDRE

I said we would find you some day but I didn't really believe it.

CHARLIE

Why not?

DEIDRE

You were married somewhere. I thought you'd soon have a family.

CHARLIE

It never happened.

DEIDRE

I didn't know that, Charlie. I didn't want her to be hurt.

CHARLIE

Where is she now?

DEIDRE

Now, she's in Paris. I came back here with her to the States when she was six, and lived in New York for a few weeks, the Italian section of Greenwich Village. But I felt like a displaced person.

CHARLIE

I can understand that. After being overseas a couple of years, I felt that way when I returned.

DEIDRE
When we were in New York she wanted to look for you. It was such a sad feeling. I just said it was a very big city.

CHARLIE
It is. When she was six? I wasn't there. I was in San Francisco.

DEIDRE
I was never comfortable in New York, so I thought it best for her to return to Rome.

CHARLIE
So, she's lived her entire life in Rome?

DEIDRE
Oh no! When she was eleven we went to the Bay Area and she attended school there, until she finished high school.

CHARLIE
That must have been difficult after growing up in Rome.

DEIDRE
She loved it. There were so many things she could do in America she couldn't do over there.

CHARLIE
What about her English? Wasn't that a problem?

DEIDRE
Her English was good but at that age she became fluent quickly.

CHARLIE
The Bay Area? Where exactly?

DEIDRE
Not far from where I bought the farm. I kept doing translation work remotely but then I got a job teaching Italian and French.

CHARLIE
I feel like I've got a lifetime of catching up to do. Tell me more about her. After high school, what did she do?

DEIDRE
She went to the Sorbonne and lived in Paris for a time, and Rome.

CHARLIE
Amazing! And then?

DEIDRE
She went back to Rome. Now she lives in Paris.

CHARLIE
She sounds restless, not able to settle down, searching for something.

DEIDRE
She leads a busy life. But yes, she thought I'd given up looking for you but she never has.

CHARLIE
Well, she can stop looking. Does she know about me now?

DEIDRE
Of course. I called her right away. She's thrilled and can hardly wait to meet you. You'll love her.

CHARLIE
I already do. What about you? Where'd you live all that time?

DEIDRE
(She smiles.) Charlie, while you were travelling all over looking for me, I was in California most of the time.

CHARLIE
I guess I'm still in shock just a bit. All this time I've had a daughter.

DEIDRE
I have to leave for an appointment, but there's something else.

They are interrupted by his cellphone. He looks at it.

CHARLIE
It's Willie. I better take it. *(He answers.)* Willie. What is it? *(He listens.)* Willie needs my help. I have to go. *(He gives her a hug.)* I'll call you as soon as I can.

He runs off. Deidre puts her hand to her forehead and weeps softly.

<u>End of Scene Two</u>.

Scene Three: *The coffee shop, several months later. Early in the day. Deidre sits with a book. She seems distracted. The waitress brings a coffee to her table, and has a cornetto in her hand.*

WAITRESS
We now have a cornetto to go with your cappuccino.

DEIDRE
(She smiles weakly and nods.) That's wonderful. Grazie.

WAITRESS
Prego.

The waitress leaves the cornetto. Charlie enters, turns to waitress.

CHARLIE
Cappuccino e croissant, per favore.

WAITRESS
Cappuccino e cornetto?

CHARLIE
(He smiles and nods.) Si. Va bene. Grazie.

WAITRESS
Prego. *(She leaves.)*

CHARLIE
When you called, I was so excited I didn't ask when you'd got back.

DEIDRE
An hour before I called, after I got my baggage. I couldn't wait.

CHARLIE
I'm so happy to see you. How was Paris?

DEIDRE
Actually, it was Rome and it was hot. And then the sirocco came. It was terrible. The wind blew straight through the house, rattling windows and opening doors. Orange dusty sand covered everything.

CHARLIE

It's been a long time. I've missed you.

DEIDRE

Charlie, I'm sorry I left on such short notice. When you went to see Willie, I didn't know then I had to leave.

CHARLIE

It's my fault for leaving so abruptly but I felt I had to help Willie.

DEIDRE

I understand. What was it?

CHARLIE

He'd fallen. I could tell he was close to tears.

DEIDRE

I'm so sorry. How is he now?

CHARLIE

He recovered from the fall, but he's gotten much weaker over the last few months. I saw him yesterday.

DEIDRE

I want to go see him as soon as I can.

CHARLIE

You'll see him soon. He's going to try to get here for a few minutes.

DEIDRE

I feel terrible I wasn't here to see Willie and to help him.

CHARLIE

I haven't heard a word from you all this time.

DEIDRE

So much has happened since I last saw you.

CHARLIE

Just before I got Willie's call, you mentioned an appointment and there was something else. Is anything wrong?

DEIDRE
There is something wrong, Charlie. I don't know where to begin.

Deidre acts confused. Charlie notices and puts an arm around her.

CHARLIE
Just start at the beginning. You had an appointment?

DEIDRE
I went to the doctor because I've been feeling strangely. And then I got a call from Rome. I had to leave immediately. I booked a standby flight, packed quickly, and headed for the airport.

CHARLIE
Whoa. One thing at a time. What about the doctor? Can you tell me?

DEIDRE
He's pretty sure I have early onset of Alzheimer's.

CHARLIE
My Lord. What made you think so?

DEIDRE
I've been forgetting things and then I got lost in Trastevere.

CHARLIE
Deidre, that's incredible. That's awful. Is the doctor sure?

DEIDRE
Pretty sure. We'll have more tests but there's not much they can do.

CHARLIE
Did they say what you can expect?

DEIDRE
It'll be a gradual process of forgetting things and getting lost or confused. I'll soon need someone to look after me.

CHARLIE
I'll look after you, until the day I die.

DEIDRE

I was just kidding, well a little, but do you mean that? Seriously?

CHARLIE

I couldn't be more serious. I don't want to lose you again.

DEIDRE

Charlie, that's not everything.

Two women come in for coffee. They order and continue talking as they stand nearby waiting for their coffee.

FIRST WOMAN

I have to admit I was wrong.

SECOND WOMAN

What do you mean?

FIRST WOMAN

I overlooked a few things at first.

SECOND WOMAN

What about? What things?

FIRST WOMAN

He didn't do anything for months but when he turned his back on so many ordinary people, I got a bit nervous.

DEIDRE

(Sotto voce.) It takes a lot to admit you may be wrong.

SECOND WOMAN

I don't understand.

FIRST WOMAN

The health care thing. That would have screwed lots of people.

SECOND WOMAN

He's lied so many times, why would you believe him on this?

FIRST WOMAN

I don't know. I thought he would keep his promises.

SECOND WOMAN
On the wall, maybe. A cockamamy idea.

FIRST WOMAN
And then the tax thing. All his rich pals benefit and screw the ordinary folk.

CHARLIE
(Sotto voce.) There's hope after all.

SECOND WOMAN
You said you'd overlook that. What convinced you not to trust him?

FIRST WOMAN
The Russia stuff.

SECOND WOMAN
What Russia stuff?

FIRST WOMAN
It's pretty clear he's been blackmailed and is doing secret deals.

SECOND WOMAN
For personal interest, or against our country? What do you mean?

FIRST WOMAN
Both. Throw the bum out. Drain the swamp.

SECOND WOMAN
Those are pretty serious charges.

FIRST WOMAN
And now he's been giving highly classified secrets away. And obstructing justice with investigations.

SECOND WOMAN
That's treason.

FIRST WOMAN
Yep. And he should be jailed, impeached, whatever.

SECOND WOMAN
Well, you've really changed your mind about him.

FIRST WOMAN
He's a corpulent corrupt clown.

SECOND WOMAN
Obese crook would be more to the point. And such a wimp.

FIRST WOMAN
How can you say that? He acts tough.

SECOND WOMAN
Didn't you see that article? He cowers from any fight, points fingers in a loss but takes credit for any win. A coward, a loser, a two-bit punk. And he hides behind those tweets.

FIRST WOMAN
I heard someone call him a fascist. What's that?

SECOND WOMAN
Never mind. Just think of him as a mob boss. But he's worse than that. He's an enabler of fascism and fascists around the world.

FIRST WOMAN
I read something by that CIA guy. I couldn't understand it.

SECOND WOMAN
You mean this? *(Shows paper.)* I brought it for you. Listen. *(Reads.)* 'When the full extent of your venality, moral turpitude, and political corruption becomes known, you will take your rightful place as a disgraced demagogue in the dustbin of history. You may scapegoat..'

FIRST WOMAN
What's venality? What's turpitude? What's ..?

SECOND WOMAN
Never mind. I think you got the idea.

FIRST WOMAN
Looks like our coffee's almost ready.

They stand quietly, waiting uncomfortably.

CHARLIE
Wow. When they turn against him, they turn with a vengeance.

DEIDRE
It's always been that way. Idols come crashing down in a hurry.

SECOND WOMAN
Speaking of obese, how's your husband doing?

FIRST WOMAN
He's not obese, just overweight.

SECOND WOMAN
Almost as bad. I read that sixty percent of us are overweight and thirty percent are actually obese.

FIRST WOMAN
That may be high. Anyway, Joe agrees with the president on this. He doesn't think exercise is all that good for you.

SECOND WOMAN
What a role model POTUS is. He thinks exercise shortens your life since you only have a fixed amount of energy.

FIRST WOMAN
At least Joe isn't a crook.

SECOND WOMAN
Does he also agree with the president that climate change and global warming are hoaxes?

FIRST WOMAN
Well, let me think. What does Fox News say?

They pause briefly from talking. Deidre starts giggling and Charlie joins her. They finally stop laughing.

SECOND WOMAN
I heard on the news some time ago that the Senator from Arizona has brain cancer. Sad. He's such a hero.

FIRST WOMAN
Isn't that what Ted Kennedy had? He went quickly.

Deidre looks grim.

DEIDRE
That's what Peter had. Glioblastoma. Invasive. Difficult to cure.

The two women get their coffee and start to leave.

SECOND WOMAN
They introduced a bill requiring a mental health exam for POTUS.

FIRST WOMAN
The House GOP will never pass it. They won't allow it.

SECOND WOMAN
He'd never pass the exam. But at least it makes many people think.

FIRST WOMAN
The Democrats would have to take over the House.

SECOND WOMAN
That could happen.

They disappear. There's silence as Charlie and Deidre watch them.

CHARLIE
I read an analysis recently saying he has signs of dementia, declining faculties, third grade vocabulary, even early Alzheimer's. Possible?

DEIDRE
Possible. He repeats and forgets what he says. I shudder to think he and I have anything in common.

CHARLIE
Before we were interrupted, you mentioned a call from Rome?

DEIDRE
The call was from Carlotta. From the hospital. She needed my help.

CHARLIE
What happened?

DEIDRE
She was in a car accident. I guess you could say she was outfurboed.

CHARLIE
You mean like furbo and fesso?

DEIDRE
That's right. Her Fiat was between two trucks as three lanes merged to two. She thought she had the edge and they thought she'd fesso.

CHARLIE
The result? Crunch?

DEIDRE
Totaled. She was taken to the hospital with multiple broken bones in her leg and wrist. She's lucky to be alive.

CHARLIE
What's the prognosis?

DEIDRE
She's in rehab. We just hope she won't be crippled for life.

CHARLIE
When will they know?

DEIDRE
She's recovering slowly. There's a good chance she'll walk again.

CHARLIE
It's been a pretty tough time, hasn't it?

DEIDRE
It could've been worse. She could've been killed.

CHARLIE
Driving in Italy is always hazardous.

DEIDRE
She'll be more fesso from now on. That is, if she can drive again.

CHARLIE
And if she gets a car. When do they think she'll get out of rehab?

DEIDRE
When she can manage on her own. But she'll be sore for a long time.

CHARLIE
Where'd you stay in Rome?

DEIDRE
You remember I told you about my aunt in Trastevere?

CHARLIE
Yes, and the wonderful neighborhood you lived in.

DEIDRE
She and her husband passed away years ago when Carlotta was in the Sorbonne. They left everything to us.

CHARLIE
I'm confused. Why did you come back? Doesn't Carlotta need you?

DEIDRE
Yes, she does. But there was something else. I had to go to Paris.

They're interrupted by seeing Willie at the door. He's been helped there and hobbles in slowly using his cane. Deidre rushes over and Charlie follows. They help him to a chair.

WILLIE
Charlie told me you were back. Am I ever glad to see you!

DEIDRE
Yes, I'm back Willie. *(She puts her arm around him.)*

WILLIE
Are you staying for a while?

DEIDRE

Yes. Why do you ask?

He takes her hand and puts it on a lump high up on his ribcage.

WILLIE

That's the tumor. Went right through my ribs. Big as an orange.

DEIDRE

Oh Willie. The pain must be excruciating.

WILLIE

Hurts like hell. The meds help a little. I'm hoping the two of you are here for the next couple of weeks.

DEIDRE

Why?

WILLIE

(Softly.) It'll be time for you and Charlie to be with me.

DEIDRE

(Gives him a hug.) Alright Willie, I'll be there.

WILLIE

Charlie, I'm afraid.

CHARLIE

Of dying?

WILLIE

Hell, no, I've had a good life. I'm afraid of being forgotten.

CHARLIE

I'll never forget you, Willie.

WILLIE

Not you. Others. Do you remember what we talked about?

CHARLIE

Yes Willie, I remember.

WILLIE

Will you make sure I'm not forgotten?

CHARLIE

I promise you, Willie, as God is my witness, I'll do everything in my power, whilst I live and breathe, that you'll not be forgotten.

WILLIE

Thanks, Charlie. Now, I have one more favor to ask. About politics.

CHARLIE

That's not important now.

WILLIE

It is to me. Please listen, Charlie.

CHARLIE

Alright.

WILLIE

I've always written about common folk.

CHARLIE

Yes, I know. Vivid. Realistic. You care.

WILLIE

I was one, Charlie. I still am.

CHARLIE

Willie, there's nothing common about you.

WILLIE

You know what I mean. I struggled all my life. I worked in a factory. I'm one of them, Charlie.

DEIDRE

What is it, Willie? What do you want?

WILLIE

Tell their story. Tell my story.

CHARLIE
Factory workers? Construction folks? Plumbers and painters?

WILLIE
Yes. People laid off. Not always working. Those people.

DEIDRE
Shopkeepers? Truck drivers? Farmers?

WILLIE
You've got it.

CHARLIE
Teachers? Small businesses struggling? Delivery workers?

WILLIE
That's it. Remember what you said about stepping into the shoes of others? Think about how they might feel?

CHARLIE
I remember.

WILLIE
There's one group of people that care only about the rich. The other group used to care about the working stiff; now many of the politicians and others have forgotten the common folk.

CHARLIE
What it's like to lose your job, your house?

WILLIE
You understand, Charlie.

CHARLIE
What it's like to be poor, to struggle for years to survive, to worry about your family, your health, to lose hope?

WILLIE
Yes. I was poor once.

CHARLIE
So was I, Willie. I know what you mean.

WILLIE

No gas for my car.

CHARLIE

(He laughs.) No car.

WILLIE

Not enough food for my family. That's why I grow most of my own.

DEIDRE

I was like that too. It's a story to be told. Many of us were once there, or still are.

WILLIE

We'll not be successful unless we stand in the shoes of average struggling families and feel what they feel, about their job, their house, their health, their pain.

CHARLIE

Their day-to-day struggle to live. I'll tell that story, Willie.

DEIDRE

I'll help him.

WILLIE

Thanks. And now, will you both help me home?

They exit with Deidre and Charlie holding Willie between them.

<u>End of Scene Three.</u>

Scene Four: *The coffee shop, early next day. Charlie enters, looks around somewhat perplexed, and sits. The waitress comes over.*

WAITRESS
Two days in a row? What'll it be this time? What language today?

CHARLIE
(He smiles briefly.) Un café et un croissant, s'il vous plaît.

WAITRESS
Avec plaisir.

The waitress leaves. Deidre enters unsteadily.

CHARLIE
I thought you'd be here before me. Are you alright?

DEIDRE
I would've been, but I lost my way coming over. Forgot for a bit.

CHARLIE
How do you feel now?

DEIDRE
I feel fine, just a little distraught over Willie. I'm so sad.

CHARLIE
I understand. *(He sees the waitress.)* Here comes our waitress. Café?

WAITRESS
Et croissant?

DEIDRE
(She nods.) Oui. Merci.

WAITRESS
Je vous en prie. *(She leaves.)*

DEIDRE
Did you see the look on Willie's face yesterday when you said he'd not be forgotten? He looked serene.

CHARLIE

Yes. *(He speaks softly.)* It was the look of a man at peace.

DEIDRE

Willie wants us with him sometime in the next couple of weeks.

CHARLIE

That won't be necessary.

DEIDRE

(She gets a puzzled look.) What do you mean?

CHARLIE

Willie's son called this morning. Willie died peacefully in his sleep.

They move together holding each other for a long moment. Deidre sheds tears. Charlie follows. She speaks softly.

DEIDRE

After you reassured him yesterday, I think he just let go.

CHARLIE

The mind's a powerful force. It often makes decisions over the body.

DEIDRE

Most of the time people just say "enough is enough". Willie was different. I think he really was at peace.

They hold each other in silence for a moment and then part.

CHARLIE

Before he walked in yesterday, you said something about going to Paris when you were in Rome. Why?

DEIDRE

It's said when one person moves out of your life, another moves in to it. When one door closes, another one opens.

CHARLIE

What do you mean by that?

DEIDRE

Charlie, you told me you always dreamed of having grandchildren. Well, you have one.

CHARLIE

What are you saying? This's no time to joke, not on that subject.

DEIDRE

I'm not joking. You have a granddaughter. Carlotta has a daughter.

CHARLIE

I have a granddaughter? That's incredible. I really do? But why didn't you tell me before?

DEIDRE

I'm sorry, Charlie. I tried to find a good time to tell you but it never seemed like the right time.

CHARLIE

What's her name?

DEIDRE

Renée and she's eight years old. She's the reason I went to Paris.

CHARLIE

She was in Paris and her mother was in Rome? Where's her father?

DEIDRE

She doesn't have a father, Charlie.

CHARLIE

Now what do you mean by that?

DEIDRE

He left when she was a baby. He's never known her. I guess you could say he fled responsibility.

Charlie is speechless, He tries to absorb all of this.

CHARLIE

Renée was in Paris and Carlotta was in Rome. I'm confused.

DEIDRE
Well, actually, Carlotta lives in Paris with Renée.

CHARLIE
But she was in Rome?

DEIDRE
She had to take a brief trip to Rome and arranged for a friend to look after Renée while she was gone. Then the accident happened.

CHARLIE
Renée was in Paris? Where is she now?

DEIDRE
I brought her back with me.

CHARLIE
She's here? Where?

DEIDRE
A friend is looking after her for a short while. She'll be here soon.

CHARLIE
You know how much this means? She knows I'm her grandfather?

DEIDRE
Yes, I told her some time ago.

CHARLIE
Do you think she'll like me?

DEIDRE
Charlie, she's wanted to meet you ever since she knew. How could she not like you? She knows I love you.

CHARLIE
And she knows I love her?

DEIDRE
Of course.

CHARLIE
Oh, Deidre.

DEIDRE
There's one more thing I have to ask.

CHARLIE
What's that?

DEIDRE
I need to go back to Rome. For Carlotta. She'll need help for some time. Especially after she's released.

CHARLIE
And you want me to look after our granddaughter?

DEIDRE
Renée.

CHARLIE
After Renée?

DEIDRE
No, Charlie.

CHARLIE
No?

DEIDRE
I want you to go back to Rome with us. I need help.

CHARLIE
I'd love to, but what do you mean? What do you want me to do?

DEIDRE
My Alzheimer's getting worse. I'm afraid of getting lost, of all sorts of things. Will you take us there?

CHARLIE
Are you kidding? I've dreamed of going there for most of my life, with you.

DEIDRE

It won't be the same, Charlie. Not as it was when we were young.

Charlie moves toward her and she responds. He holds out his hand.

CHARLIE

It'll be wonderful. We'll have cappuccinni e cornetti, sitting in the piazza in the morning sun.

DEIDRE

And stroll through the streets together, hand in hand? *(Takes his.)*

CHARLIE

And see the Caravaggio and Cavallini paintings in the churches.

DEIDRE

And dine together in the late warm summer evenings, listening to the music of Rome?

CHARLIE

I'll look after you from now on, Deidre.

DEIDRE

And Renée?

CHARLIE

And Renée.

DEIDRE

And help me look after our daughter until she recovers?

CHARLIE

Carlotta.

DEIDRE

And Carlotta?

He nods. They move closer, and she reaches up to kiss him. They are interrupted by seeing Renée and Deidre's friend at the door. Renée releases the friend's hand, waves goodbye to her, and then strides purposefully and confidently toward Deidre and Charlie.

DEIDRE

Renée, this is your grandfather.

RENÉE

Je le sais, Mamie. *(She turns to him.)* Bonjour. Je m'appelle Renée.

CHARLIE

Je le sais, Renée. Enchanté.

Renée takes his hand with one hand and Deidre's with the other, walks between them, taking them toward the exit.

RENÉE

Let's go home.

Renée leads them, firmly, one on each side. She looks straight ahead, in command. They look down at her, then at each other and smile. They exit.

End of Scene Four.

End of Play. Curtain call.

www.ingramcontent.com/pod-product-compliance
Lightning Source LLC
Chambersburg PA
CBHW031309060426
42444CB00033B/1085